# LEARN TO PLAY
# EASY PIANO CLASSICS

## Philip Hawthorn

**Edited by Jenny Tyler and Helen Davies**

**Designed by Philip Hawthorn and Kim Blundell**

**Illustrated by Joseph McEwan and Guy Smith**

**Additional illustrations by Peter Dennis**

**Music arrangements by Daniel Scott and Caroline Phipps**

**Series editor: Anthony Marks**

**Music engraving by Poco Ltd., Letchworth, Herts**

# Contents

# Introduction

The tunes in this book are taken from popular pieces of classical music, and have been specially arranged and simplified to make them easy to play. Many of them should be familiar, even those with titles that you may not recognize. The pieces are grouped in three sections according to the period in which they were written. At the beginning of each section there is an introduction to the music and composers of that period.

## Naming and numbering pieces of music

Most pieces of music have a number, called an opus number. (Opus is the Latin word for "work"). In the 17th century, composers began to number their works as they were published, opus 1 (or op.1), opus 2 and so on. Often a single opus number was given to a group of pieces published together in one book. When several pieces appeared with the same opus number, each one was given a second number, for example, op.1, no.4.

Composers often gave their music titles as well. For example, Beethoven called his sixth symphony the Pastoral Symphony. Sometimes titles were added later by other people. Beethoven's sonata op.27, no.2 was given the name Moonlight Sonata.

# The Baroque period

Baroque is the name given to the European style of art, architecture and music from about 1600 to 1750. Buildings were very ornate, and music echoed this. Baroque music started in Italy, and worked its way north to Germany, France and England. It is known for its contrasts of speed and volume.

Many new styles or forms of music were developed in the Baroque period, some of these are described here. On the opposite page you can find out about the Baroque composers whose music appears in this section.

## Oratorios and cantatas

An oratorio is a musical story or drama, usually on a religious theme. It is performed by a choir and orchestra without costumes, scenery or action. Cantatas are similar to oratorios but they are more an act of worship, often including popular hymn tunes.

## Opera

An opera is like a play where some or all of the words are sung. The first operas were staged in private homes in the 1590s by a group of poets and composers called the Camerata. The first public opera house (a special theatre for opera) was opened in Venice in 1637.

## The concerto grosso

In the Baroque period, a type of piece called the concerto grosso was popular. It was written for a small group of instruments and a larger orchestra. The orchestra acted mainly as an accompaniment, while the smaller group played special solo parts.

## Dance music and suites

Baroque composers began to use dance music in their works. An example of this is the minuet, a dance which was very popular at the court of Louis XIV in France.

A suite is a group of pieces of music, often including several different dance styles.

## The first piano

Early piano

Harpsichord

The first piano was made in about 1700 by an Italian called Cristofori. Pianos didn't really become popular, though, until later in the 18th century. Until then, the main keyboard instruments were the harpsichord, virginal, spinet and clavichord. Only on the clavichord were the strings struck, as they are on a piano. The others had quills to pluck the strings.

## The orchestra

For the Orchestra 1750
Violins 12
Violas 6 } strings
Cellos 6
Double Basses 6
Oboes 2
Bassoons 2 } Wind
Horns 2
Harpsichord 1 or 2 } Continuo
Also available ~ Trumpets and drums for festive occasions
Recorders for French and Venetian Opera
Trombones for Church music.

Example of a baroque orchestra.

An orchestra is a large group of instruments. In the Baroque period, an orchestra had up to around 40 players. More than half of the instruments in an orchestra are strings. There are also sections of brass, woodwind and percussion instruments. Baroque orchestras were directed by the harpsichord player or the lead violinist.

# Baroque composers

### Henry Purcell
### (1659-1695)

Purcell was the most famous English Baroque composer. He had a song published when he was eight, and at 20 became the organist at Westminster Abbey in London. He wrote over 500 works, including music for 40 plays. He also wrote for royal occasions such as coronations, and the funeral of Queen Mary in 1695.

### Tomaso Albinoni
### (1671-1751)

Albinoni was an Italian composer. He wrote over 40 cantatas, many concertos and a lot of other instrumental music, mainly for strings. He also wrote over 50 operas. He lived most of his early life in Venice, where he opened a singing school with his wife, Margherita, in 1709. After her death, he directed his operas all over Europe.

### Antonio Vivaldi
### (1678-1741)

Vivaldi was an Italian composer who also trained to be a priest. From 1703 he taught the violin at a girls' school in Venice. He is best known for his development of the concerto, and wrote about 550 of them for various instruments. Although he was a famous musician for much of his life, he died a poor man.

### George Frideric Handel
### (1685-1759)

Handel was born in Germany. His father didn't want him to be a musician, so as a boy he had to play in secret. He lived in Italy for a while, then went to England and became a British subject in 1726. He composed for kings George I and George II. Handel wrote many kinds of music, including oratorios, operas and concertos.

### Johann Sebastian Bach
### (1685-1750)

Bach was born into a famous German musical family, and held important posts as a musician at the courts of Weimar and Cöthen. He was an excellent organist, violinist and harpsichord player. His music later influenced many other composers, including Mozart, Beethoven and Mendelssohn.

### Thomas Arne
### (1710-1778)

Arne was one of the most famous English composers of the late 18th century. He was noted for writing pleasant melodies. He wrote over 30 operas, and lots of music and songs for plays, including those of Shakespeare. The tune for which he is best remembered is now known as *Rule, Britannia* .

# Trumpet Tune

Purcell wrote many anthems and voluntaries in this style, though many of them were lost.

His music was in great demand in both the theatre and the church.

**Purcell**

# When I am laid in earth

This tune is from the opera *Dido and Aeneas*. It is based on *The Aeneid*, a story by the Roman poet Virgil.

It is also called *Dido's Lament* and is sung before she dies.

**Purcell**

# Adagio

When Albinoni died, he left a lot of music unfinished. In 1945, an Italian named Giazotto listed all of Albinoni's music.

Giazotto thought this piece was so beautiful that he completed it.

**Albinoni/Giazotto**

# Spring

This is one of four violin concertos called *The Four Seasons*. Each is based on a poem.

*The Spring has come, and joyfully is greeted by the birds with happy song,*

On the left you can see how the poem for *Spring* begins.

**Vivaldi**

9

# Alla Danza (from Water Music)

This tune is from the second movement of the *Water Music suite in D*. It was written for George I of England in 1717.

This music was composed for a royal river outing on the Thames.

**Handel**

Allegro moderato

## Writing music down

During the middle ages, the words of a song had small marks, called neumes, over them. These showed roughly how high or low the notes were (the pitch).

Guido of Arezzo, an Italian monk who died in 1050, perfected the staff, which showed the exact pitch of notes. The example on the right is from the 13th century.

Handel also wrote some music for a fireworks display given by George II in 1749, to celebrate peace after the war of Austrian Succession.

At the first performance in London, the wooden frame built to support the fireworks caught fire.

Many people contributed to the development of music notation. In the 13th century Franco of Cologne first used different symbols to show notes of different lengths.

On the left is a piece of music by the French composer Josquin des Près (1440-1521). It was written near the end of the 15th century.

# Arrival of the Queen of Sheba

This tune is from the oratorio *Solomon*, based on a story in the Old Testament of the Bible.

It was written in 1749, and first heard at Covent Garden, London.

**Handel**

Handel's best known religious oratorio is probably *Messiah*, written in 1742. It is about the life of Christ.

On the left you can see a page from the original music. The words, or libretto, were written by a man called Jennens.

# Thine be the glory

This piece was originally from Handel's oratorio called *Judas Maccabaeus*. It is now better known as a hymn tune.

The picture shows some of Handel's pupils in England – the Prince of Wales and his sisters. **Handel**

# Canon in D

Pachelbel was born in Germany in 1653. He was a successful composer and organist.

The picture shows St. Stephen's Cathedral in Vienna, where Pachelbel was an organist for five years.

Andantino

**Pachelbel**

# Viola concerto in G

Telemann (1681-1767) was born in Hamburg, Germany. This theme is from the first movement of the concerto.

Telemann and his friends used to meet in coffee houses to play music and socialize.

**Telemann**

# Brandenburg concerto no.3

This theme is from the first movement of the concerto. Bach wrote six Brandenburg concertos.

It is not known exactly when they were written, but they were completed by March, 1721.

**Bach**

# Air on a G string

This tune is from Suite no.3 in D. Suites are groups of pieces, usually dance tunes.

The bass part, with its regular, stepwise pattern of notes, is typical of Baroque music.

**Bach**

Bach was a very fine organist and wrote a lot of organ and church music. After his death, his music went out of fashion for about 80 years.

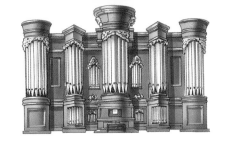

On the left is a picture of the organ he used at the New Church at Arnstadt in Germany.

# Minuet in G

Bach wrote this tune for his second wife, Anna Magdalena. She was a professional singer. They were married in 1721.

The picture shows the cover of a book of music which Bach dedicated to her.

**Bach**

# Rule, Britannia

This is a song from a masque called *Alfred*, written in 1740. A masque is a sort of play with music, singing and dancing.

Masques were popular at the houses of wealthy noblemen.

**Arne**

# The Classical period

Some people call all serious music "classical", but the word is mainly used to describe the music of the second half of the 18th century. Classical music reflects the confidence and prosperity of this period. New instruments enabled composers to develop new sounds, harmonies and musical forms. Some of these forms are explained below. At this time, Vienna was one of the most important musical cities. Haydn, Mozart and Beethoven, the three greatest composers of the age, lived there for much of their lives.

## The symphony

A symphony is a piece of music for an orchestra. In the Classical period, most symphonies had four sections, called movements. Each one had its own speed and style, often in the pattern shown below.

1. Fairly fast and lively.

2. Slow

3. A minuet and trio (dance tunes).

4. Fast and cheerful.

## The concerto

A concerto is a piece of music for an orchestra and a soloist. It developed from the Baroque form, the concerto grosso (see page 4). The concerto usually had three movements, like those shown below.

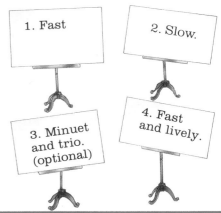

1. Fast. Usually the orchestra begins and then the soloist joins in.

2. Slow.

3. Fast.

In the first and last movements, the soloist sometimes had a part to play alone, called a cadenza.

## The sonata

Classical sonatas were written for either a single keyboard instrument, or for a keyboard and one other instrument. They usually had three or four movements (see below).

1. Fast

2. Slow.

3. Minuet and trio. (optional)

4. Fast and lively.

## The Classical piano

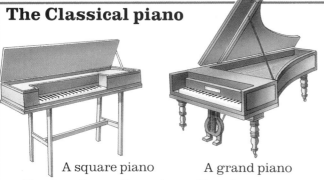

A square piano          A grand piano

During the 18th century, the piano gradually grew in popularity. Unlike the harpsichord, it could play loudly (forte) and softly (piano). This meant that a much wider variety of music could be played on it.

In the 18th century, Cristofori's invention was called the "fortepiano". Later, it became known as the pianoforte, and eventually it was shortened to just the piano. Today, the word Fortepiano is used for an instrument built in the early 18th century.

## Orchestras

23 violins

7 violas

5 cellos

2 clarinets

3 bassoons

drums

7 double basses

5 flutes and oboes

4 horns

2 trumpets

2 harpsichords

As new instruments were invented or developed, orchestras grew in size. Above you can see the most common orchestral instruments of the classical period, though others were frequently included as well. Orchestras were usually still directed by the harpsichord player or lead violinist.

# Classical composers

## Franz Joseph Haydn (1732-1809)

Haydn was born in Rohrau, Austria. He trained as a choirboy, and sang in the choir of St. Stephen's Cathedral in Vienna for ten years. In 1766, he became music director at the court of the Esterházys, a rich Hungarian family. He worked for them, on and off, for most of his life. Haydn wrote nearly every form of music, including 108 symphonies, many string quartets, operas and church music.

His music was popular all over Europe. He visited many major European cities, including London. In the 1780's he became very good friends with Mozart (see below), who dedicated a set of string quartets to him.

## Wolfgang Amadeus Mozart (1756-1791)

Mozart was an Austrian composer, and wrote his first music at the age of five. At seven he went on a concert tour of Europe. Above you can see a poster for a concert he gave in England.

Mozart wrote his first symphony at the age of nine. He lived in Salzburg, Paris and Munich, but settled in Vienna in 1781. He often appeared as the soloist and conductor for his own music.

Mozart wrote a huge amount of music, including 41 symphonies, 27 piano concertos, religious music, chamber music and 19 operas. Above is a scene from his opera *The Magic Flute*.

## Ludwig van Beethoven (1770-1827)

Beethoven was born in Bonn, Germany, where his father and grandfather were both musicians. From 1792, he lived in Vienna. His early pieces included the Moonlight Sonata for piano, three piano concertos, and two symphonies.

From about 1802, he was troubled by gradual and incurable deafness. But he continued writing all kinds of music. Because of pieces like his third, fifth and sixth symphonies, the opera *Fidelio* and two more piano concertos, he became known as the greatest composer of his day.

By the end of his life he was almost totally deaf, but this was when he wrote some of his greatest music. His last string quartets contain some of the most challenging music ever written. In his ninth symphony, he used a choir as well as an orchestra, to increase the dramatic effect of the music.

Beethoven's ear trumpets

# Bourrée

Leopold was the father of Wolfgang Amadeus Mozart. He was also a musician.

The picture on the left shows Salzburg, the city where Leopold Mozart lived and worked.

**Leopold Mozart**

Moderato

*f*

# Che farò

Gluck was a German composer. He studied in Prague and he also lived in Vienna and Milan.

This song is from an opera called *Orfeo ed Euridice*. The picture shows a scene from the opera.

**Gluck**

# Emperor's hymn

This and the next tune are from a set of six string quartets, op.76. This is the third, called *The Emperor*.

Arms of Austrian Empire

West German flag

It was originally the Austrian national anthem, and is now the anthem of West Germany.

**Haydn**

# String quartet in D
## op.76, no.5

A string quartet is music played by a cello, a viola and two violins. This tune is the fifth in the set.

The op.76 string quartets were written in 1797.

**Haydn**

# Clarinet concerto

Mozart loved the sound of the clarinet. He wrote this concerto for his friend Anton Stadler, a famous clarinettist.

A clarinet in Mozart's time.

This tune is from the second, slow, movement.

**Mozart**

# Romance
## (from Eine Kleine Nachtmusik)

The title of this music is German. It means "a little night music". It was completed in 1787.

This form of music is called a serenade. It would often be played after a dinner.

**Mozart**

29

# Symphony no.40

This symphony is one of Mozart's last. Parts of it are very sad and moving.

This is the first tune, or theme, in the symphony.

**Mozart**

Mozart's last three symphonies, numbers 39, 40 and 41, were written in six weeks during 1788.

On the left is a picture of Mozart conducting an orchestra.

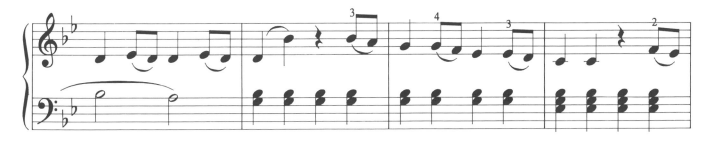

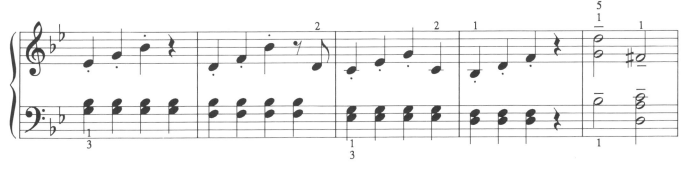

## Amazing pianos

Ever since the piano was invented, there have been many weird and wonderful ones made. You can see some on the right.

A piano that could also be used as a table, made about 1850.

A "twin semi-cottage" piano (made about 1850) had two keyboards for two players.

A "harp piano" made in 1857.

# Duet from The Magic Flute

The Magic Flute is one of the last pieces Mozart wrote. This duet is sung by the characters Papageno and Pamina.

Papageno is the royal birdcatcher.

It is sung just as Papageno rescues Pamina from the evil Monostatos.

**Mozart**

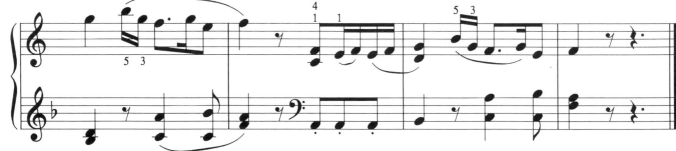

# Ode to Joy

This tune comes from Beethoven's ninth symphony. It is called the Choral Symphony because it was the first one to include a choir.

Beethoven's birthplace in Bonn, Germany.

By the time it was performed Beethoven was too deaf to hear the music or the applause.

**Beethoven**

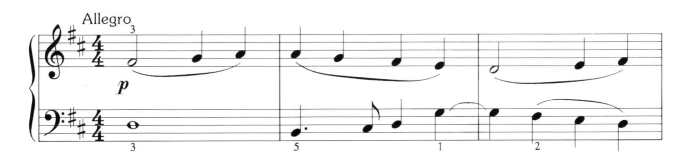

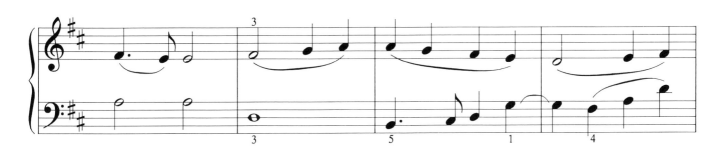

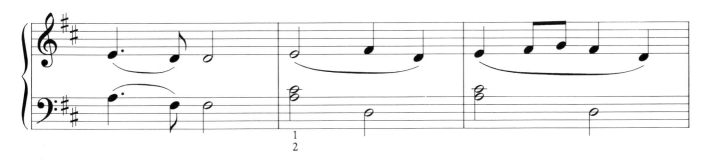

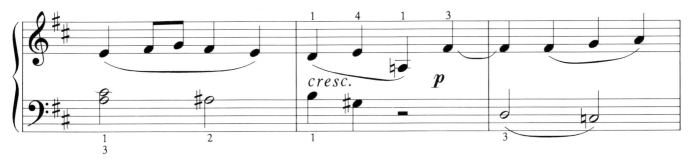

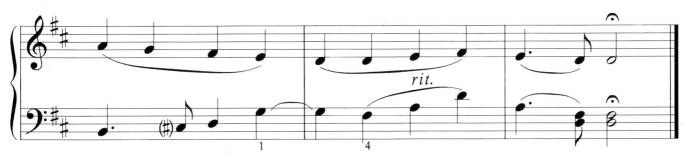

# Pastoral Symphony

This symphony was Beethoven's sixth. It is based on the theme of the countryside.

The tune is from the first movement.

**Beethoven**

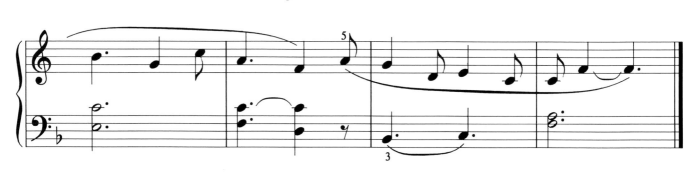

# Minuet in G

A minuet is a dance tune in three-four time.

The picture shows a piano quintet (a piano playing with a string quartet).

**Beethoven**

# Moonlight Sonata

This sonata (op.27, no.2) was written in 1801. It was dedicated to a Countess with whom Beethoven was in love.

It got its name because a poet called Rellstab said it reminded him of moonlight on a lake.

**Beethoven**

On the right is
the last page of
the original
manuscript for
the Moonlight
Sonata.

Beethoven played the
piano at the first
performances of much
of his piano music. On
the left is a picture of
his grand piano.

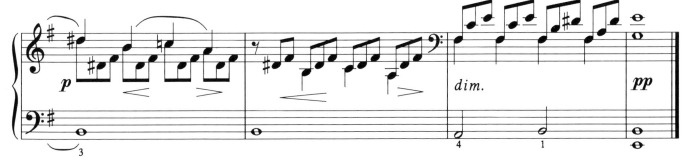

# The Romantic period

'Romantic' is the word used for a new style of music that developed in Europe in the 19th century. It was often inspired by other arts, especially poetry and painting. Romantic composers tried to write music that expressed their feelings and emotions, and much of their work is very dramatic and moving.

Some people view Beethoven as the first Romantic composer; he introduced Romantic styles and expressions into his later music. He was followed by Schubert and then many others. You can find out about them on the opposite page. Romantic composers, especially when they performed as well, were often very popular and had huge followings. You can find out more on page 54.

## The orchestra

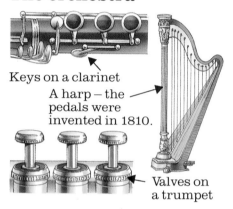

Keys on a clarinet

A harp – the pedals were invented in 1810.

Valves on a trumpet

By about 1830, the orchestra looked more or less like it does today. There could be anywhere between 70 and 100 instruments, depending on the type of music. Many instruments were improved by the invention of valves and keys (see above). The harp was also included in orchestras from about 1820.

As orchestras grew larger, it was no longer practical for one of the musicians to direct the others and play at the same time. Since the eary 19th century, most orchestras have been directed by a separate musician called a conductor.

A conductor stands in front of the orchestra, beating time with one hand, and telling the orchestra how loudly or softly to play with the other. The introduction of a conductor meant that very precise directions could be given to the orchestra.

As a result, composers began to write more complex music with greater variation in dynamics and tempo. The conductor was able to control the speed, volume and mood of the music very accurately, so composers began to be more adventurous in the kind of music they wrote for the orchestra.

## Romantic music

During the Romantic period, many different types of music were popular. On the right, you can read about some of the most important Romantic styles.

## The Romantic piano

During the Romantic period, the piano became the most popular instrument. It was much more strongly built, so its sound was able to fill the large concert halls that were being built. It was also given more keys. In the picture below you can see an upright piano.

These were first produced on a large scale in the 1870s and were the kind most people had in their homes.

Songs called Lieder, especially those of Schubert.

Piano pieces which expressed a mood (Chopin's Nocturnes).

Music for ballets, for example, that of Tchaikovsky.

Opera – with exotic settings and romantic or adventurous plots.

# Romantic composers

**Franz Schubert (1797-1828) Austrian**

Schubert was known mainly as a writer of songs, but he also composed beautiful instrumental music, such as the *Trout Quintet.*

**Nicolò Paganini (1782-1840) Italian**

Paganini was not only a composer, but also a virtuoso performer. He played the violin to wildly enthusiastic audiences.

**Gioachino Rossini (1792-1868) Italian**

Coming from a musical family, Rossini wrote his first opera at 18. He composed 40 more, including *The Barber of Seville.*

**Hector Berlioz (1803-1869) French**

Berlioz was a very inventive composer. He was also a very emotional man, and this is reflected in much of his music.

**Robert Schumann (1810-1856) German**

A gifted pianist, Schumann wrote piano and orchestral music. He composed over 300 songs, many influenced by his love for his wife, Clara.

**Felix Mendelssohn (1809-1847) German**

Mendelssohn was a pianist and conductor as well as a composer. He played and conducted his music all over Europe.

**Fryderyk Chopin (1810-1849) Polish**

Chopin was one of the greatest composers of piano music. He influenced many others, including Liszt, Tchaikovsky and Grieg.

**Franz Liszt (1811-1886) Hungarian**

Liszt was a brilliant concert pianist by the age of 12. His piano music is among the most difficult ever written.

**Giuseppe Verdi (1813-1901) Italian**

Almost all Verdi's music is opera. He wrote and directed all over Europe. Among his best known are *Aïda*, *La Traviata* and *Rigoletto*.

**Richard Wagner (1813-1883) German**

Much of Wagner's music was political. He was banished from Germany for 11 years. His 4 operas called *The Ring of the Nibelung* last 18 hours.

**Johannes Brahms (1833-1897) German**

Brahms wrote a wide variety of music, including four symphonies and many songs. He was a close friend of Schumann.

**Camille Saint-Saëns (1835-1921) French**

Saint-Saëns was a famous pianist, organist and composer. He was admired by Liszt and influenced many others, including Ravel.

**Pyotr Il'yich Tchaikovsky (1840-1893) Russian**

Tchaikovsky is famous for many types of music: symphonies, concertos, and ballets such as *Swan Lake* and *The Nutcracker.*

**Edvard Grieg (1843-1907) Norwegian**

Grieg promoted Norwegian music as a composer, pianist and conductor. Two famous works are the *Piano Concerto*, and *Peer Gynt*.

**Giacomo Puccini (1858-1924) Italian**

After seeing Verdi's *Aïda*, Puccini dedicated himself to opera. Among his best known works are *La Bohème* and *Madam Butterfly.*

# Impromptu op.142, no.3

An impromptu is meant to sound as if it is being improvised, that is, made up on the spot.

The picture on the left shows Schubert's room with his piano.

**Schubert**

40

# The Unfinished Symphony

This symphony, Schubert's eighth, only has two movements. It is thought he didn't finish it because he got tired of it.

A statue of Schubert in Vienna, Austria.

It wasn't performed until 37 years after Schubert's death.

**Schubert**

# Serenade

This piece is the music to a song. Schubert wrote over 600 songs, called Lieder.

 ← One of Schubert's song manuscripts.

 On the left is the front page of a song which Schubert wrote, called *The Trout.*

**Schubert**

# Caprice no.24

A caprice is a light-hearted piece of music written to be played in a carefree style.

Paganini wrote this piece for the violin. He was a brilliant and popular violinist.

**Paganini**

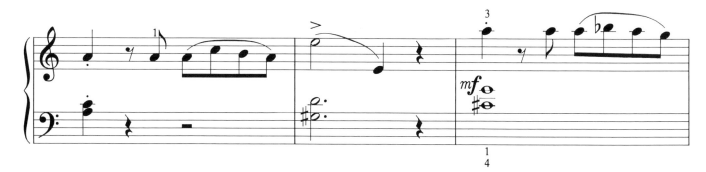

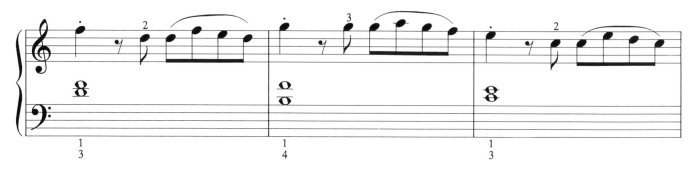

# William Tell overture

An overture is the instrumental music which introduces an opera or oratorio. Rossini wrote the opera *William Tell* in 1829.

The picture shows characters from an 1844 production at London's Covent Garden.

**Rossini**

# Harold in Italy

This piece has a solo viola part that Berlioz wrote for Paganini. In fact, Paganini never played the piece.

Berlioz was also a famous conductor.

It is based on a poem by the poet Byron called *Childe Harold's Pilgrimage.*

**Berlioz**

# The Jolly Peasant

This tune is from a set of piano music called *Album for the Young*. It was written in 1848.

This is the town of Leipzig, where Schumann studied.

**Schumann**

# The Wild Horseman

This tune is also from Schumann's *Album for the Young*. He wrote many pieces with descriptive titles.

Robert and Clara Schumann at the piano

Schumann's wife, Clara, was a concert pianist and music journalist.

**Schumann**

For a while, Chopin lived in Paris (shown on the right).

# Prelude
## op.28, no.7

Although he was a very talented pianist, he gave very few public performances.

**Chopin**

# Nocturne op.9, no.2

A nocturne is a piano piece which is quiet and thoughtful. The name is from the word nocturnal, meaning "of the night".

Chopin's birthplace near Warsaw, Poland.

Chopin was inspired by John Field, an Irish composer who wrote nocturnes in the early 19th century.

**Chopin**

Chopin was a brilliant pianist. He often composed music by improvising at the piano.

On the left is a picture of Chopin at the age of 19, playing for Prince Radziwill in Berlin.

# Violin concerto in E minor

Mendelssohn wrote this concerto for his friend Ferdinand David, a violinist. This tune is from the second movement.

The picture shows Mendelssohn, aged 11, playing for the writer, Goethe.

**Mendelssohn**

Mendelssohn wrote many kinds of music, including concertos, sonatas, piano works and dramatic music.

His music was very popular with the English aristocracy, and he was invited to many social gatherings.

# Liebesträume

*Liebesträume* means "dreams of love". Liszt gave the title to the piano arrangements of three of his songs.

The *Liebesträume* are nocturnes.

Liszt as an old man, in his study.

**Liszt**

## Famous musicians

During the 18th century, audiences often ate, drank and talked during concerts. In the Romantic period, audiences listened more carefully. Some soloists had many fans, a bit like modern pop stars.

Paderewski played in London in 1892.

The Polish pianist Paderewski (1860-1941) was often mobbed by audiences during his concerts. In 1919, he became the president of Poland.

# La donna è mobile

This song is from an opera called *Rigoletto*. It was first performed in 1851.

This opera is about a court jester. The picture shows costume designs for the first production.

**Verdi**

## The story of Rigoletto

There is gossip that Rigoletto (the Duke of Mantua's jester) has a lover hidden away. In fact he is keeping Gilda, his daughter, hidden from the world, only allowing her out on Sundays, to go to church. She is in love with a stranger she has seen there (the Duke).

Some of the Duke's men kidnap Gilda, to prove that Rigoletto has a secret lover. In a rage, Rigoletto pays an assassin to kill the Duke, but the assassin's sister falls in love with the Duke. She refuses to let her brother kill him, but they must kill someone to give Rigoletto a body and claim the fee. To save the Duke's life, Gilda allows herself to be killed, and her body is placed in a sack. When Rigoletto opens it, he finds the body of his daughter.

# Ride of the Valkyries

This is from the opera *The Valkyrie*. It is the second of four that make up the opera cycle called *The Ring of the Nibelung*.

The picture shows the Valkyries. They were the daughters of Wotan, the chief of the Gods.

**Wagner**

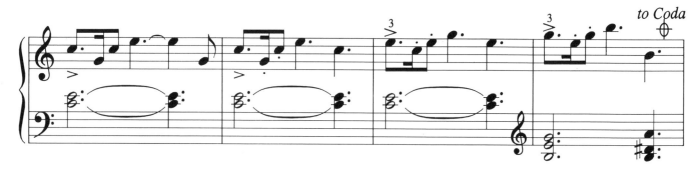

# Bridal chorus

This popular wedding march is from the opera *Lohengrin*. It is played when Lohengrin, Knight of the Grail, marries Elsa.

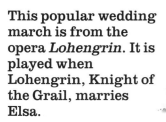

Wagner wrote the libretto for the opera, as well as the music. He finished it in 1850.

**Wagner**

# Symphony no.3

The tune below is from the third movement. In the symphony (first heard in 1883) it is played by the cellos.

Brahms was an excellent pianist. On the left is a picture of him playing.

**Brahms**

# Swan Lake

*Swan Lake* is a ballet, written in 1877. The swans in the story turn into beautiful maidens.

This tune is for the first appearance of the swans.

**Tchaikovsky**

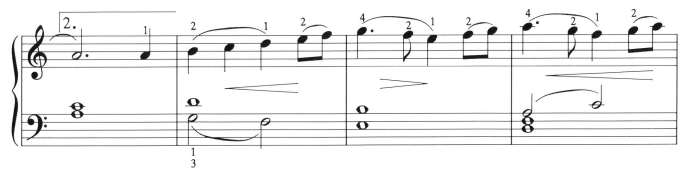

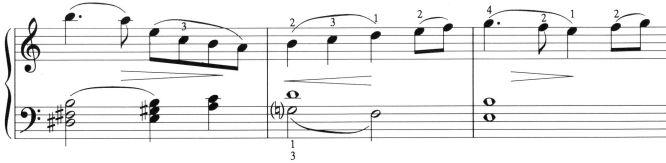

# Piano concerto no.1

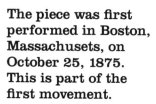

The piece was first performed in Boston, Massachusets, on October 25, 1875. This is part of the first movement.

On the left is the booklet handed to the audience at the first performance.

**Tchaikovsky**

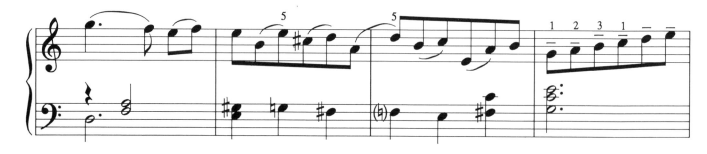

# Solveig's song

Solveig's song is
from a play called
*Peer Gynt*, by the
Norwegian writer
Henrik Ibsen.

Grieg

The tune is based on
a Norwegian song.
Grieg was very fond
of folk music.

**Grieg**

# Playing the pieces

On these two pages you will find some hints on how to play the pieces in this book. When you are learning a piece, it is usually better to practice each hand separately at first. When you can play each hand comfortably, try to play them at the correct speed, and then try playing both hands together.

There are suggestions for fingerings in the music, but you can try to work out your own fingerings if these do not feel comfortable. If you want to start with the simplest pieces in the book, look at Minuet in G on page 20, and the Pastoral Symphony on page 34.

## Trumpet tune

Try to keep an even, marchlike rhythm.

## When I am laid in earth

There are lots of accidentals in this piece, especially in the third line. Practice each hand on its own at first, until you are confident of the notes.

## Adagio

This piece is slow, so make sure the triplets are even. Take care in the first and second time bars - you might want to practice these separately at first.

## Spring

The right hand plays thirds almost all the way through this piece. Practice until you can play them accurately.

## Alla Danza (from Water Music)

The opening chords in the right hand are difficult. Practice these until you are confident of the fingering.

## Arrival of the Queen of Sheba

This is very fast, so practice the right-hand part until you can play it at the correct speed before adding the left-hand part.

## Thine be the glory

You may find it easier to practice this in sections. There are six sections in the piece, each four bars long.

## Canon in D

Familiarize yourself with the fingering in the left hand before trying both parts together.

## Viola concerto in G major

The first two bars on the last line are a bit tricky, so they may need a little extra work.

## Brandenburg concerto no.3

Take care with the fourth line, as there are some big leaps in the right hand.

## Air on the G string

Keep the left hand very steady throughout the piece. There are lots of large leaps, so you will need to practice this on its own before adding the right hand.

## Minuet in G

Take care not to rush - play at a relaxed tempo.

## Rule, Britannia

Make sure you are confident of the fingering in the right hand before trying both hands together.

## Bourrée

Play this very smoothly.

## Che farò

Keep the left-hand part flowing evenly.

## Emperor's hymn

When both hands are playing the same rhythm, make sure you keep them absolutely together.

## String quartet in D op.76, no.5

When the left hand is playing quarter note chords in the last two lines, make them softer than the right hand to allow the tune to come through.

## Clarinet concerto

In the last three lines of the piece, make sure you play the thirds in the left hand very smoothly.

## Romance (from Eine kleine Nachtmusik)

Take care with the sixteenth note passages in the third and fourth lines. The fingering is sometimes a little tricky here.

## Symphony no.40

Play the left hand part a little softer than the right hand, so that you can hear the tune clearly. Keep a steady pace in the left hand, especially in the first two lines of the first page and the first three lines of the second page.

## Duet from The Magic Flute

From the second bar of the second line to the first bar of the third line, the left hand has the tune. Play the right-hand part a little softer in these bars.

## Ode to Joy

Play this very steadily, evenly and confidently.

## Pastoral Symphony

Play the chords in the left hand very softly. Make sure you hold each one for its full length.

## Minuet in G

Take care with the passages in thirds in the right hand. Practice these on their own until you can play them without any mistakes before adding the left-hand part.

## Moonlight Sonata

Play this very quietly and smoothly. Make sure you keep the triplets even throughout.

## Impromptu op.142, no.3

Practice the rhythm in the left hand before trying both hands together. This rhythm gives the piece its character, so try to play it as smoothly as possible.

## Unfinished Symphony

The tune is in the left-hand part, so play this a little stronger than the right hand. Be careful not to make the chords in the right hand sound too heavy.

## Serenade

Make sure you don't rush the triplet here. Try to play it exactly in time.

## Caprice no.24

This is fairly fast, so practice the right-hand part until you can play it fluently before playing both parts together.

## William Tell overture

Keep the chords in the left hand fairly short, making sure you leave a full quarter note rest between each one.

## Harold in Italy

Play this very smoothly.

## The Jolly Peasant

You may find the first two bars on line two a little difficult at first. Play them a few times until you get used to the rhythm.

## The Wild Horseman

Pay particular attention to the staccatos and slurs in this piece.

## Prelude op.28, no.7

The right-hand part is fairly difficult, so practice it very slowly at first.

## Nocturne op.9, no.2

Practice the second line on the second page on its own before trying the whole piece. Some of the notes will need careful practice.

## Violin concerto in E minor

This piece is fairly difficult, so you should practice both parts until there are no mistakes, before trying them together. The last three lines may need a little extra work.

## Liebesträume

The eighth notes in the right hand should be a little softer than the dotted half notes, as these are really part of the accompaniment.

## La donna è mobile

The staccato chords in the left hand should be played very lightly.

## Ride of the Valkyries

Pay particular attention to the accents in this piece, and emphasize the dotted eighth notes.

## Bridal chorus

Try not to rush this. You should keep a fairly moderate pace throughout.

## Symphony no.3

Practice the right-hand part of the first and second time bars on its own, until you are confident of the rhythm. The number "5" over the notes means that you play five sixteenth notes in the time of four. Try to play them as evenly as possible.

## Swan Lake

Take care with the fingering in lines two and three.

## Piano concerto no.1

The fourth line is fairly difficult, so you should practice this on its own before playing the whole piece.

## Solveig's song

There are a lot of accidentals in the fourth and fifth lines. Play both parts until you are confident of the notes in these two lines, before putting both parts together.

# Index

First published in 1994 by Usborne Publishing Ltd, Usborne House, 83-85 Saffron Hill, London EC1N 8RT, England.

AE. First published in America in August 1994
Printed in Portugal